Dear Parent:
Your child's love of reading starts here!

Every child learns to read in a different way and at his or her own speed. You can help your young reader improve and become more confident by encouraging his or her own interests and abilities. You can also guide your child's spiritual development by reading stories with biblical values and Bible stories, like I Can Read! books published by Zonderkidz. From books your child reads with you to the first books he or she reads alone, there are I Can Read! books for every stage of reading:

SHARED READING
Basic language, word repetition, and whimsical illustrations, ideal for sharing with your emergent reader.

BEGINNING READING
Short sentences, familiar words, and simple concepts for children eager to read on their own.

READING WITH HELP
Engaging stories, longer sentences, and language play for developing readers.

READING ALONE
Complex plots, challenging vocabulary, and high-interest topics for the independent reader.

ADVANCED READING
Short paragraphs, chapters, and exciting themes for the perfect bridge to chapter books.

I Can Read! books have introduced children to the joy of reading since 1957. Featuring award-winning authors and illustrators and a fabulous cast of beloved characters, I Can Read! books set the standard for beginning readers.

A lifetime of discovery begins with the magical words "I Can Read!"

Visit www.icanread.com for information on enriching your child's reading experience.
Visit www.zonderkidz.com for more Zonderkidz I Can Read! titles.

People who refuse to work
want things and get nothing.
But the longings of people who work hard
are completely satisfied.
— Proverbs 13:4

ZONDERKIDZ

Pirate in Training
Copyright © 2012 by Big Idea, Inc. VEGGIETALES.® character names, likenesses and
other indicia are trademarks of Big Idea, Inc. All rights reserved.

Requests for information should be addressed to:
Zondervan, 5300 *Patterson Ave SE, Grand Rapids, Michigan 49530*

ISBN 978-0-310-73207-5

Editor: Mary Hassinger
Art direction: Kris Nelson
Cover design: Karen Poth
Interior design: Karen Poth

Printed in China

12 13 14 15 16 /DSC/ 22 21 20 19 18 17 16 15 14 13 12 11 10 9 8 7 6 5 4 3 2 1

ZONDER**kidz**

Pirate in Training

story by Karen Poth

The pirates were tired.

They played games

all day.

"Let's go take a nap,"

the pirates said.

Inside the ship,

the pirates fell asleep.

A noise from on deck

woke them up.

Knock! Knock! Knock!
Someone was knocking
on the ship's door.

"Go away," said Pa Grape.
"We are sleeping."

KNOCK! KNOCK! KNOCK!

"We should see who is there," Larry said.

"It could be a cow bringing lunch."

The pirates LOVED lunch.

"It could be a boy scout

with yummy candy," Pa Grape said.

"Or … maybe Spaceman Stan is here
to take us on an adventure!"
Larry was excited!

Larry opened the door.

But … there was no yummy candy.

There was no cow with lunch.

There was no

Spaceman Stan.

It was Junior Asparagus at their door.

"Hi fellas," Junior said.

"I want to be a pirate, just like you."

Junior jumped in the pirates' beds.

"Why do you want to be a pirate?"

asked Mr. Lunt.

"School is too hard," Junior said.

"I'm tired of working."

"I want to play games

and nap all day," said Junior.

"Starting today,

I am a Pirate in Training!"

Junior smiled.

"Being a pirate

IS a lot of work," Larry said.

"Even pirates go to school,"

Mr. Lunt told Junior.

"We use math to add up

food bills," said Larry.

"And we have to read a map
to sail the seven seas!" he added.

"To be a good pirate,
you must go to school."

"And while you're in school
you might even see
there are some other things
you'd like to be!" Pa said.

Junior could
be a policeman,
with a badge
and a light.

Or a cowboy
with a BIG hat
and a rope!

Or maybe even a SPACEMAN

flying through space!

"If you work hard in school,"

Pa Grape told Junior,

"you can be anything

God wants you to be!"

31

Junior thought.

Then he ran for the door.

"I'm late for school," he said.

"I will be back for pirate

training this summer!"